Cloud Native Networking Deep-Dive

T0074261

Published 2023 by River Publishers
River Publishers
Alsbjergvej 10, 9260 Gistrup, Denmark
www.riverpublishers.com

Distributed exclusively by Routledge
605 Third Avenue, New York, NY 10017, USA
4 Park Square, Milton Park, Abingdon, Oxon OX14 4RN

Cloud Native Networking Deep-Dive / by Chander Govindarajan, Priyanka Naik.

© 2023 River Publishers. All rights reserved. No part of this publication may be reproduced, stored in a retrieval systems, or transmitted in any form or by any means, mechanical, photocopying, recording or otherwise, without prior written permission of the publishers.

Routledge is an imprint of the Taylor & Francis Group, an informa business

ISBN 978-87-7004-021-1 (paperback)

ISBN 978-10-0381-022-3 (online)

ISBN 978-1-032-62821-9 (ebook master)

A Publication in the River Publishers series
RAPIDS SERIES IN COMMUNICATIONS AND NETWORKING

While every effort is made to provide dependable information, the publisher, authors, and editors cannot be held responsible for any errors or omissions.

Cloud Native Networking Deep-Dive

Chander Govindarajan

IBM Research, India

Priyanka Naik

IBM Research, India

River Publishers

Routledge
Taylor & Francis Group

NEW YORK AND LONDON

7.4 k8s-netsim: Multi-cluster Networking 59

7.5 Summary 63

8   Retrospective   **65**

Index   **67**

About the Authors

Chander Govindarajan is a Research Engineer at IBM Research, India with 5 years' experience in the field of systems ranging from Blockchain, Telco-Cloud and multi-cloud networking, working in the intersection of academic research and business interests. Prior to joining IBM Research, he completed his Dual-Degree in CSE from IIT Kharagpur.

Priyanka Naik is a Research Scientist at IBM Research, India. Her area of interest lies in optimizing the deployment of containerized network functions. She is currently working on multi-cloud networking and aspects around frameworks for edge and cloud connectivity. Prior to joining IBM she obtained her Ph.D. from IIT Bombay, India. Her thesis revolved around easing building and monitoring of network functions deployed on cloud.

Figure 1.1: A glimpse of the network topology we will simulate in this book.

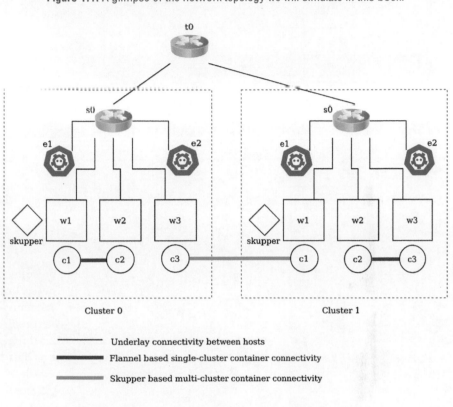

Let's get started.

Introduction to Kubernetes Concepts

In this chapter, we take a brief look at some Kubernetes concepts. The reader may ignore this chapter completely if they are aware of and have used Kubernetes before.

The concepts of cloud and cloud computing have evolved over the past several decades. It was realized in the 1950s that there is a need to have sharing of compute, memory, disk, and resources to be more cost efficient, which led to the introduction of *mainframe computers*. Further, the need for time sharing across geographies was handled by the introduction of ARPANET, the ability to communicate systems at different locations, i.e. the birth of Internet. The resource sharing demand increased and so in 1972 IBM introduced *Virtual Machine OS*. The virtual operating system ran over the existing operating system but was dedicated to a particular user. This enabled sharing of resources on a machine in an isolated environment which was used on IBM mainframes. In the 1990s, along with isolation, system resources like compute, disk, memory, and isolation in a network was provided with help of "virtual" private networks as a rentable service.

The era of what we know today as cloud computing began in the 2000s with Amazon's AWS and Google's doc application hosted on their infrastructure, shared/editable across users in any geography in real-time. Companies like IBM and Google collaborated with universities to build large server farms or data centers to build the infrastructure required to run these cloud applications. They had orchestration platforms like Openstack[1] and F5[2] to run virtual

---

[1]https://www.openstack.org/
[2]https://www.f5.com/

Figure 2.1: Kubernetes architecture.

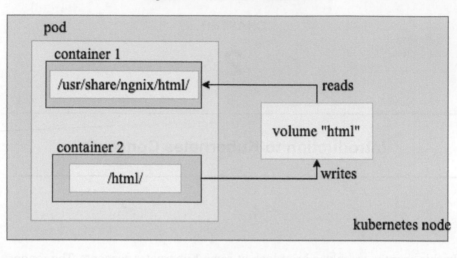

machines for various users and their applications. A virtual machine based cloud infrastructure provided isolation but had performance overheads due to an additional layer of a guest operating system. Containers helped fill the gap of providing isolation in a shared infrastructure without the additional OS overhead. Since 2013, *Docker* containers have become the de facto to deploy applications on such containers on a single machine. In 2017, to enable container deployment on a large cloud infrastructure *Kubernetes* was launched as a cloud native (container) orchestration platform. This chapter will cover the various concepts in Kubernetes that enabled this wide acceptance in the cloud community.

Kubernetes[3] or *k8s* is a container orchestration platform that provides features like automated deployment, scaling, and security for the applications. It has components like a controller and scheduler to manage the spawn of the containers and manage scaling, as shown in Figure 2.1. The basic unit in k8s is *pod* which is an logical host for an application. A pod comprises of a group of containers with a shared storage and network. For example, as shown in Figure 2.2, there can be a two containers running a pod with container 1 acting as a web server and generating some response and fetching data from the shared volume in which it is fetched from a remote server by container 2 running MongoDB. A sample YAML config to create a pod is as shown in Listing 2.1. There are also some specific containers that can run as part of the application

---

[3]https://kubernetes.io/

Figure 2.2: Pod architecture.

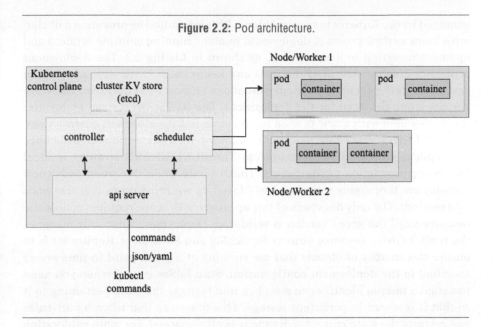

running as a pod. *Init containers* are part of the app pod and the application container starts only after init containers finish execution. This helps enable a dependency chain across micro-service chains where there are some config dependencies between the micro-services and the order of them is critical. *Sidecars* are another example of containers running along with the application container to handle tasks such as monitoring, logging, and update config on the fly.

```
apiVersion: v1
kind: Pod
metadata:
  name: nginx
spec:
  containers:
  - name: nginx
    image: nginx:1.23.4
    ports:
    - containerPort: 80
```
Listing 2.1: Example pod YAML

In Kubernetes terminology, pods are hosted on a worker or a node. The node can be a physical server or a virtual machine. The lifecycle of the pods is managed by the Kubernetes control plane. This is handled by providing a declarative know as *deployment*. A deployment enables running multiple replicas and updating/reverting to new versions, as shown in Listing 2.2. The deployment controller monitors status of the pods and keeps them in the desired state. In case of errors the events in the deployment can be used to fix the issue. There are various strategies used for the deployment. The RECREATE strategy restarts the deployment with a new version for example in a development environment. The ROLLING UPDATE helps smooth migration with old version removed once the replicas with new versions are up. The BLUE/GREEN strategy is ideal for testing/production environments. That is, only when the green pods (new version) are thoroughly tested and validated do we bring down the blue pods (old version). The only drawback of this approach is that one requires double the resource until the green version is validated. Deployment internally manages the replicas using resource objects *ReplicaSet* and *StatefulSet*. ReplicaSet is to ensure the number of objects that are running at a given point in time are as specified in the deployment configuration. StatefulSet is used when you need to assign a unique identifier to a replica and manage the state pertaining to it so that it is stored in persistent storage. This to ensure that when a particular pod restarts the state corresponding to it is also restored. For more exploration one can also refer to instructions available[4].

```
apiVersion: apps/v1
kind: Deployment
metadata:
  name: nginx-deployment
  labels:
    app: nginx
spec:
  replicas: 3
  selector:
    matchLabels:
      app: nginx
  template:
    metadata:
      labels:
        app: nginx
    spec:
      containers:
      - name: nginx
        image: nginx:1.23.4
```

---

[4]https://kubebyexample.com/concept/deployments

```
ports:
- containerPort: 80
```

Listing 2.2: Example deployment YAML

Since deployment helps manage the application pod's lifecycle, scaling the pod's cluster IP changes on restarts. However, a client needs a static IP and endpoint to access the microservice. *Service* is used to expose the the application (see Listing 3.3). There are various service types:

- *Cluster IP*: Used for accessing an application internally in a cluster using a cluster IP as a service IP.
- *NodePort*: Expose service using the node IP and a static port on the node.
- *Load balancer*: Expose the service using the cloud based load balancer. This helps for application with multiple replicas.
- *External name*: Add a name to the service (eg. xyz.com).

```
apiVersion: v1
kind: Service
metadata:
  name: serviceA
spec:
  selector:
    app.kubernetes.io/name: App1
  ports:
  - protocol: TCP
    port: 80
    targetPort: 9080
```

Listing 2.3: Example service YAML

These services now form a higher layer abstraction that can be used safely without worrying about where or how many pods are being run. Later in this book, we shall see how this is achieved.

Finally, now that we have Services running in a cluster that can talk to services, we need an additional layer of control in exposing these services outside the cluster. This is needed not just from a security point of view, but also from a standard application management viewpoint.

There are a lot more pieces in Kuberenetes that we have not touched upon here. The introduction here is very light on purpose and we invite readers who don't know about Kubernetes to take some time now to read more into it. The training available on the official website[5] may be a good place to start.

---

[5]https://kubernetes.io/training/

CHAPTER

3

Workers and Containers

In this chapter, we shall start with the very basics of running a container cluster orchestrator, which is running the worker/host nodes and containers on them. In this chapter, our containers will not be able to talk to each other yet; this is something we will add in subsequent chapters.

3.1 Workers in Kubernetes

Kubernetes clusters are typically composed of a number of "workers" that form the basis of the compute cluster, off the shelf computing machines or VMs, which form the host for running containers on top of.

Hosts can either run standard operating systems distributions based on Linux such as Ubuntu or Redhat Enterprise Linux (RHEL) or can run custom stripped down versions built for this purpose such as Core OS[1] or Flatcar[2]. The role of the host is similar to the Hypervisor in the traditional VM virtualization clusters, in that it sets up required resources like disk and underlying networking, and enables the creation and management of containers on top.

Worker nodes are connected to each other over switches and routers – the exact networking between them depends on the placement of the workers in the data center and their types. If they are themselves virtual, then there are at

---

[1]https://fedoraproject.org/coreos/
[2]https://www.flatcar.org/

least two layers of networking already (apart from the new layers that we shall examine deeply in this book).

3.2 Simulating Workers

In our simulation, we do not care about the exact configuration of the workers or the networking between them – these details are not relevant when trying to understand container networking.

We use Mininet – a network emulation tool – to simulate multiple workers and then work on top of these simulated workers. In the next section, we talk briefly about what Mininet is.

3.3 Technology: Mininet

Mininet[3] is a well established tool for creating virtual networks used for research development of new algorithms such as for switching and routing and used in academia for teaching networking. Using simple commands, users can launch virtual networks running real kernel and switch codes managed by real SDN controllers like Open vSwitch. Mininet has an easy to use CLI which enables the creation of nodes and links, and supports network libraries for ping, tcpdump, etc. Also, for any component created in the Mininet network you can run your custom code for it. Thus, Mininet is beneficial for working on new protocols and network topology, and is a great tool for a learning networking.

Written in Python, Mininet internally uses a process based virtualization that scales well to large topologies on a single machine. Mininet uses network namespaces to manage individual entities (we shall dig deeper into this technology in this chapter), but understanding the details of Mininet is not needed to understand the approach in this book. As part of this book, we use a Mininet-based topology to understand cloud networking.

3.4 k8s-netsim: Workers

As mentioned earlier, since we are interested in container networking to a large extent we do not care about the exact network topology used in the layers below – as long as workers can connect to each other.

---

[3]http://mininet.org/

For simplicity, in our simulator, we go with a very simple approach: we model worker nodes of a cluster as Mininet hosts all connected to a single switch. That is, workers in our cluster are in a single L2 domain. Note that this is quite an ordinary construct, nodes in a single rack in a data center are connected to a single top of rack (ToR) switch.

Later in the book, when we have multiple clusters, we model this by connecting various cluster switches to a single top level switch.

This network (within a cluster and across) may be called an "underlay network". Note that this is distinct from the network we will create in the next chapter – between containers.

Thus, in our approach, we do not model any routers or more complicated topologies in the underlay network, since there is no need of any of this complexity.

When we run the simulator using the command:

```
$ docker run -it --privileged --rm --name knetsim knetsim
```

you will see a number of printed statements that results in a prompt that looks like:

```
*** Creating network
*** Adding hosts:
C0e1 C0e2 C0w1 C0w2 C0w3 C1e1 C1e2 C1w1 C1w2 C1w3
*** Adding switches:
C0s0 C1s0 t0
*** Adding links:
(C0e1, C0s0) (C0e2, C0s0) (C0s0, t0) (C0w1, C0s0) (C0w2, C0s0) (C0w3,
  C0s0) (C1e1, C1s0) (C1e2, C1s0) (C1s0, t0) (C1w1, C1s0) (C1w2, C1s0)
  (C1w3, C1s0)
*** Configuring hosts
C0e1 C0e2 C0w1 C0w2 C0w3 C1e1 C1e2 C1w1 C1w2 C1w3
*** Starting controller

*** Starting 3 switches
C0s0 C1s0 t0

... (output truncated)

mininet>
```

This is because the structure of our simulator is to setup a Mininet topology of workers, do a lot of other things (the rest of this book) and finally run the Mininet CLI. This CLI allows users to interact with the topology and run commands on hosts, etc.

Let us do so now and examine the network created by our simulator. By default, we have two clusters with three workers each – the six workers run as Mininet hosts with the names: C0w1, C0w2, C0w3, C1w1, and so on.

This is the syntax to run commands on workers – "<worker name> <command>".

```
mininet> C0w1 ifconfig
```

You should see an output like the following:

```
C0w1-eth0: flags=4163<UP,BROADCAST,RUNNING,MULTICAST>  mtu 1500
    inet 10.0.0.3  netmask 255.0.0.0  broadcast 10.255.255.255
    inet6 fe80::b047:2fff:fe86:2cd  prefixlen 64  scopeid 0x20<link>
    ether b2:47:2f:86:02:cd  txqueuelen 1000  (Ethernet)
    RX packets 386  bytes 52898 (52.8 KB)
    RX errors 0  dropped 0  overruns 0  frame 0
    TX packets 344  bytes 47274 (47.2 KB)
    TX errors 0  dropped 0 overruns 0  carrier 0  collisions 0

... (truncated)
```

This is the default underlay network setup by Mininet.

Exercise: verify that the underlay is working and that you can ping one worker from another. Specifically, check the ip of C0w1 and run the ping command as "ping <ip>" from the second worker.

For example, for the run above:

```
mininet> C0w2 ping 10.0.0.3
PING 10.0.0.3 (10.0.0.3) 56(84) bytes of data.
64 bytes from 10.0.0.3: icmp_seq=1 ttl=64 time=0.085 ms
64 bytes from 10.0.0.3: icmp_seq=2 ttl=64 time=0.027 ms
64 bytes from 10.0.0.3: icmp_seq=3 ttl=64 time=0.072 ms
64 bytes from 10.0.0.3: icmp_seq=4 ttl=64 time=0.030 ms
64 bytes from 10.0.0.3: icmp_seq=5 ttl=64 time=0.102 ms
...
```

When you are done, pressing Ctrl-D or "exit" in the prompt will shut down the simulator with output like the following:

```
*** Stopping 0 controllers

*** Stopping 12 links
............
*** Stopping 3 switches
C0s0 C1s0 t0
*** Stopping 10 hosts
C0e1 C0e2 C0w1 C0w2 C0w3 C1e1 C1e2 C1w1 C1w2 C1w3
*** Done
Cleaning up loose ends...
```

Exercise: try to extend the k8s-netsim to implement other underlay network topologies. Examine whether anything covered in this book changes: it will not!

3.5 Simulating Containers

In this book, we are only interested in the networking aspects of a container. So, we will simulate containers using only "network namespaces".

Our "container" will thus share process id, file system, and all other resources with the underlying host. There is no isolation guarantees in our setup (apart from networking, that is) by design.

3.6 Technology: Network Namespaces

Namespaces are one of the core technologies underlying containers. They allow an isolated, fresh view of a single sub-system comprising the resources but completely independent of the host. The various types of namespaces provided by the Linux kernel are:

- User namespace: process can have root privilege within its user namespace.
- Process ID (PID) namespace: Have PIDs in namespace that are independent of other namespaces.
- Network namespace: have an independent network stack (with routing rules, IP address) as shown in Figure 3.1.

Figure 3.1: Network namespace.

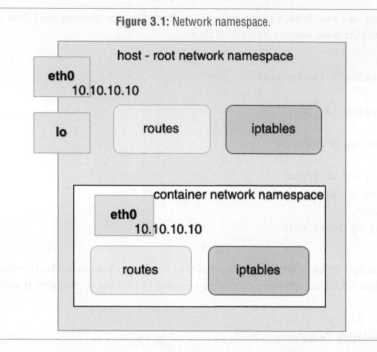

- Mount namespace: have mount points without effecting host filesystem.
- IPC namespace: IPC provides isolation for inter-process communication related objects to allow identification of the shared objects.
- UTS namespace: manages isolation of hostname and domain name. Changes made to these are visible only to processes in the given namespace.

As discussed above (Figure 3.1), since we require isolation for network interfaces and routing tables we will be using network namespaces extensively in this book. The next section describes how network isolation is achieved using the "ip netns" command.

3.7 Hands On: Network Namespaces

Let us explore network namespaces. Start a prompt as follows:

```
$ docker run -it --privileged --rm --entrypoint bash knetsim
```

This runs our docker image as a container without running the simulator. This loads an environment that is already setup with the needed tools. Alternatively, you can run commands in this section on any Linux host.

First, check the root namespace:

```
$ ifconfig
```

to orient yourself with the root network namespace.

Check the current list of namespaces using the command:

```
$ ip netns list
```

This should be empty for now.

Now, create a new namespace:

```
$ ip netns add myns
```

Run the list command above to verify that the new namepace has been created.

We can now run arbitrary commands inside our new namespace using the following syntax:

```
$ ip netns exec myns <command>
```

Run "fconfig" inside this network namespace and verify that it is different from the root namespace.

In fact, you will notice that the new net namespace is empty of interfaces. This is the expected behavior. Let us bring up the lo interface inside this namespace:

```
$ ip netns exec myns ip link set lo up
```

Now, ping localhost from the root namespace and examine the counter reported by ifconfig. Do the same inside the network namespace and check that the two counters are completely independent.

When we are done, we can delete the net namespace:

```
$ ip netns del myns
```

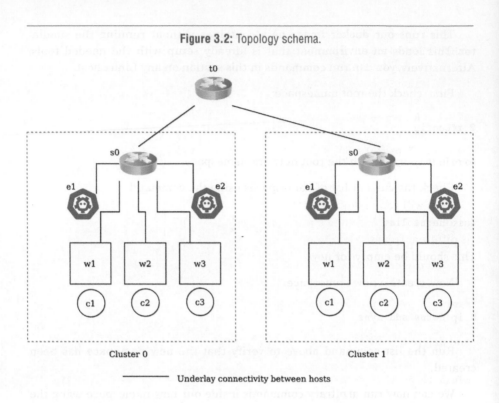

Figure 3.2: Topology schema.

------- Underlay connectivity between hosts

3.8 k8s-netsim: Containers

Hopefully, the previous section has given you an idea of network namespaces. In our simulator, each container on a worker is a new network namespace created on the worker host. Before a deep dive into how the connectivity in the topology exists, let us discuss the various components in the topology, as shown in Figure 3.2. We emulate two clusters, cluster 1 and cluster 2, each having a underlay switch (s0), and assume some connection between them, say via switch t0. Each cluster has three workers, w1, w2, w3, and each has a container/pod (c1, c3, c3 respectively) deployed on it.

By default, the simulator comes with a container "ci" running on worker "wi".

Startup the simulator and run commands in the container using the following syntax:

```
mininet> py COw1.exec_container("c1", "ifconfig")
eth0: flags=4163<UP,BROADCAST,RUNNING,MULTICAST>  mtu 1450
        inet 11.11.32.2  netmask 255.255.240.0  broadcast 11.11.47.255
        inet6 fe80::1c72:67ff:fe81:6a91  prefixlen 64  scopeid 0x20<link>
        ether 1e:72:67:81:6a:91  txqueuelen 0  (Ethernet)
        RX packets 21  bytes 1874 (1.8 KB)
        RX errors 0  dropped 0  overruns 0  frame 0
        TX packets 30  bytes 2236 (2.2 KB)
        TX errors 0  dropped 0 overruns 0  carrier 0  collisions 0
```

You will get an ouput as shown. We will see in the next chapter how IPs are assigned to the container, but for the moment check that the IP of the container is different from the worker.

You can create new containers with the following syntax:

```
mininet> py COw1.create_container("c10")
```

and delete them with the following command:

```
mininet> py COw1.delete_container("c10")
```

Note: in a real Kubernetes environment, we don't usually worry about which worker node runs which container. However, in this simulator, to keep things simple, we let the users worry about where which container runs.

3.9 k8s-netsim: Running Multiple Shells

While following through the rest of the book, you may want to run multiple shells simultaneously onto various workers and containers. The "Mininet" CLI provided by the simulator only allows a single command at a time which can be limiting.

To open different shells concurrently, you can use the following commands.

Run a shell in the simulator container:

```
$ docker exec -it knetsim bash
```

Inside the simulator environment, the following command:

```
$ ./utils/exec 0 w1
0:w1>
```

opens a shell into worker w1 in cluster 0.

Similarly, the following command:

```
$ ./utils/exec 0 w1 c1
0:w1:c1>
```

will open a shell into container c1 running on worker w1 in cluster 0.

You may find this approach much easier to play with the simulator. In the rest of this book, we use this and recommend you do the same. We also use the prompt convention to represent where to run commands. If you see a code block that starts with a prompt like ":w1> ", it means you need to exec into w1 of cluster 0. Similarly for ":w1:c1> " means that you should exec into c1 on w1 of cluster 0 using the shown command.

3.10 Aside: Pods vs. Containers

As you may have seen in the introduction chapter and elsewhere, Kubernetes deals with pods as the smallest unit of abstraction. A pod is composed of multiple containers running together.

For simplicity, in this book, we consider pods and containers as one and the same. How is this acceptable? This is because all containers within a pod share the same network namespace. Since our containers are nothing more than network namespaces, this works out very well for us.

3.11 Summary

In this chapter, we have introduced the concepts of "Mininet" and "network namespaces" and demonstrated how we run workers and containers in our simulator.

So far, our containers are running, but they cannot really talk to each other. In the next chapter, we introduce container networking – or how pods are assigned IPs and how Kubernetes allows containers to talk to each other.

4

Container-container Networking

4.1 Introduction

In the previous chapter, we saw how when new network namespaces are created, they are completely empty of any interfaces. This is true for real containers running on Kubernetes too. Then, how do we make containers talk to each other?

Specifically, in this chapter, we will try to enable the red lines that we see in Figure 4.1.

We can think of three things that need to be done after a container comes up:

- An interface has to be assigned to the network namespace, like "eth0".
- This interface has to be assigned an IP address.
- Packets coming from a pod has to be routed to other pods.

How does Kubernetes do all this?

4.2 Container-container Metworking in Docker

If we take a step back, we realize that the same problem holds for Docker containers. How is this different to Kubernetes?

Figure 4.1: In the last chapter, we got the squares and circles connected with the black lines. Red lines show connectivity between containers in a single cluster. We achieve this using the Flannel CNI plugin in this chapter.

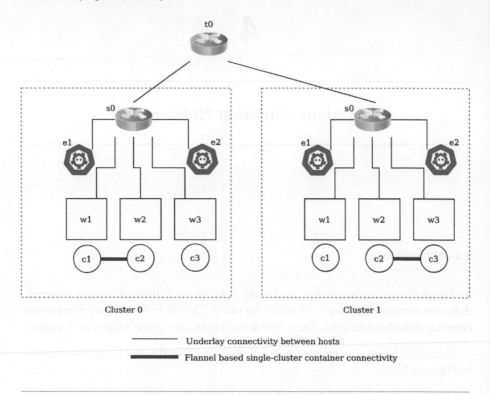

The difference is: standard Docker containers run on a single worker. Kubernetes containers run on different workers, themselves connected with an underlay.

Docker networking is achieved in a variety of ways using different drivers, but the default approach is known as "bridge". Let us look into it briefly in this section.

Docker bridge networking works using a simple model, as shown in Figure 4.2:

1. Docker creates a virtual bridge device on the host, usually known as "docker0". 2. For every container that docker creates, it creates a "veth" pair of devices. One end of the veth is inside the container (i.e. attached to the network namespace), while the other end is attached to the bridge device.

Figure 4.2: Docker networking.

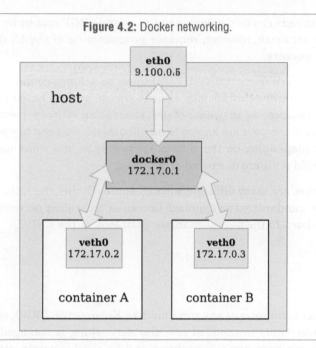

3. Packets entering one of the veth pair exits the other. 4. The bridge device acts as a simple L2 bridge and switched packets from all attached interfaces to all other attached interfaces.

This simple approach works for local containers but, as you can see, this cannot be extended to multiple workers.

4.3 Multi-host Container–Container Networking Techniques

If you abstract away the problem, there are many techniques to achieve multi-host networking.

One set of techniques known as *overlays* or *tunneling* achieve this by setting up per host pair tunnels to overlay traffic between workers. In this approach, once the tunnels are setup, the underlying host and network are unaware of the traffic routing in the overlay. One commonly used tunneling technique is VXLAN – used to setup virtual LAN – partitioning sub networks on a real LAN.

Another set of techniques, instead, bring these new endpoints as first class members of the underlay network. BGP is an example of this approach, where the new containers can be connected to the existing BGP routers by advertising routes. This approach, however, requires programming of the L3 devices that connect the workers.

Thus, there are many different techniques to achieve container–container networking. Different clusters may want to choose options based on trade-offs such as performance, security, ease-of-use, interfacing with other workloads, etc. On top of this, since pods are known to be ephemeral, we need to update routes, tunnels, etc (depending on the chosen approach) as and when new pods are created and old pods are destroyed or removed.

Since, there are many different ways to approach this, the Kubernetes community has a standardized an approach known as "container network interface" or CNI[1] for short. In the next section, we shall look at the CNI.

4.4 CNI

Any container running over any run time like Kubernetes, CRI-O, or Mesos has certain requirements in terms of how the networking is managed for it. The requirement can vary across containers and be similar across runtimes. CNI *container network interface* assists this by providing a specification and support for plugins to configure the container network, as shown in Figure 4.3. Some plugins can, for example, (i) be a bridge to help creation of an interface for a container and support intra-host communication, (ii) create an overlay using vlan, (iii) assign IP addresses: static, DHCP based, host-local. The benefit of having these plugins is one can chain these together based on the networking requirements. For example, a bridge plugin for interface, vxlan for overlay and a bandwidth plugin to add limits to the bandwidth utilization. CNI comprises of a specification , a json file to specify the network requirements, and plugins to handle them. Some meta plugins widely used today are:

- *Flannel*: This is the default CNI for Kubernetes. Flannel[2] provides layer 3 network between containers across multiple nodes. That is, it handles the inter node connectivity and supports additional plugin for inter node connectivity. We will build our own flannel based plugin as part of this chapter.

---

[1]https://www.cni.dev/
[2]https://github.com/flannel-io/cni-plugin

Figure 4.3: Container network interface.

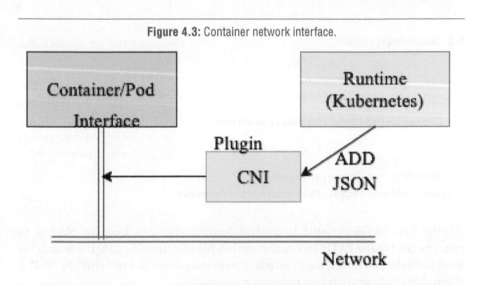

- *Cilium*: Cilium[3] is an eBPF based solution that along with networking supports observability and security. One can add L3-L7 network policies using Cilium. Since, it's built on eBPF it also supports adding dynamic code at various hook points in the kernel.
- *Calico*: Calico[4] is also an eBPF based network and policy enforcement CNI that helps choose the network dataplane between vanilla Linux, and eBPF based, and DPDK based VPP. Calico is popular for its performance and scalibility.

4.5 k8s-netsim: CNI

Now that we have seen how Kubernetes organizes its container networking, let us look at how we achieve it in our simulator. We try to run our setup as close as possible to reality, so we also run a CNI plugin, specifically Flannel to configure networking for our containers.

The real Kubernetes setup has mechanisms to call the CNI plugins when it creates and deletes containers. However, we don't have a real scheduler or orchestrators – just function calls that creates containers (that is, network namespaces).

To do this, we use a tool provided by the CNI project called cnitool.

---

[3]https://cilium.io/
[4]https://www.tigera.io/tigera-products/calico/

4.6 Technology: cnitool

"cnitool" is a development aid that allows you to run CNI plugins for a specific network namespace. You can check the documentation[5] for more details.

The typical usage of the tool is as follows:

```
CNI_PATH=/opt/cni/bin
NETCONFPATH=/tmp/knetsim/<name>
cnitool add|del <name> /var/run/netns/<nsname>
```

The CNI_PATH variable is used to control where to look for plugins to run. The NETCONFPATH has configuration files for specific plugins (which we shall see below). Finally, the "cnitool" command allows you to "add" or "del" a particular configuration in a network namespace.

4.7 k8s-netsim: Flannel

We shall use a rather standard and famous CNI plugin called Flannel in our setup. Before we get into how the networking itself works, let us look at the logistics of how flannel is deployed. Normally, this is a task done on cluster setup by Kubernetes administrators, but here we shall manually run the pieces in our simulator. This process will make it much clearer on what is configured when.

1.   A "FlannelD" binary runs as a DaemonSet (meaning one on each worker node) to manage per worker configuration. We will run the process directly on our Mininet host.
2.   "FlannelD" daemons connect to the cluster "etcd" setup to share and synchronize configuration. Etcd is a distributed key-value store used to manage a lot of the configuration across masters and workers in a Kubernetes cluster. Since we don't have the default out-of-the box etcd cluster, we run our own two node cluster – running as two new hosts in the Mininet topology.
3.   "Flannel" CNI plugin binary installed and available on each worker. Now, whenever containers come up or go down, this plugin is called. We make this plugin available on all of our worker hosts.

Now, that we have seen the pieces, what is the exact startup sequence in our simulator?

---

[5]https://www.cni.dev/docs/cnitool/

1. Cluster wide configuration is loaded into etcd first. This includes global configuration such as IP ranges, what inter-worker connectivity option to use, etc.
2. "FlannelD" daemons are started on each worker. These daemons read global configuration from etcd and generate per worker configuration.
3. Setup CNI configuration to be used for containers on all workers. This is the file to be used by cnltool to know which plugins to run.
4. Containers can now be created and deleted.

The cluster wide configuration file is available in "conf/flannel-network-config.json" and looks like the following:

```
{
    "Network": "11.0.0.0/8",
    "SubnetLen": 20,
    "SubnetMin": "11.10.0.0",
    "SubnetMax": "11.99.0.0",
    "Backend": {
        "Type": "vxlan",
        "VNI": 100,
        "Port": 8472
    }
}
```

This configuration file specifies a few global options for this cluster:

1. We specify a container network of "11.0.0.0/8" for all containers managed by Flannel. This means all containers will be assigned IPs of the form "11.xxx.xxx.xxx" in this cluster.
2. The next few options talk about subnets. Each worker is assigned a different subnet to use for containers running on it. This allows a clean partition of IPs across workers, so there is no assignment conflict and it becomes easy to route packets between workers.
3. The next few lines specify the backend to use. This is the technology used to connect containers across workers. In this example, we use VXLAN tunnels between workers. The configuration specifies the virtual network identifier (VNI) and port to use to setup the tunnels.

Notice that we use the same configuration in our simulator for all clusters. Each cluster thus will have containers assigned to the same IP ranges. This is generally acceptable, since containers form a virtual network and solutions like Flannel are only concerned with connecting containers within a cluster.

Once this configuration is loaded into the cluster etcd and all FlannelDd daemons are started up, each daemon generates a local configuration. This can be found in the path "/tmp/knetsim/<worker>/flannel-subnet.env" in the simulator environment where worker names are of the form "C0w1", "C0w2", etc.

The file looks something like the following:

```
FLANNEL_NETWORK=11.0.0.0/8
FLANNEL_SUBNET=11.10.224.1/20
FLANNEL_MTU=1450
FLANNEL_IPMASQ=false
```

(the exact contents of this file will vary between workers and runs).

The second line indicates that this FlannelD has carved out the subnet "11.10.224.1/20" for use for containers on this worker.

Exercise: Look at the running containers in the worker and confirm that the IP falls within the subnet. Create a few new containers and see that this constraint is always respected. Check the subnets of all workers and see that they are non-overlapping.

Finally, let us look at the CNI configuration being used on one of the workers:

```
{
  "name": "COw1",
  "type": "flannel",
  "subnetFile": "/tmp/knetsim/COw1/flannel-subnet.env",
  "dataDir": "/tmp/knetsim/COw1/flannel",
  "delegate": {"isDefaultGateway": true}
}
```

The "type" field is used to convey to the user ("cnitool" in this case) to search for a binary named "Flannel" to use as the CNI plugin. The "subnetFile" is the same file we saw above. The "dataDir" is used to store any other generated files etc.

The "delegate" field is used to pass params to other CNI plugins being called. This is important, since Flannel automatically creates configuration to call the "bridge" and "host-local" plugins to manage single-host networking. These are CNI plugins that come out of the box and operate much like their Docker counterparts. Here, we set "isDefaultGateway" true to enable routing of all traffic from the container through the Flannel provided bridge network. This is needed since (as we saw earlier), our network namespaces are otherwise empty of interfaces.

This is happening because Flannel is using VXLAN tunnels between the workers – specifically via the "flannel.100" virtual devices – the tunnel endpoints. Thus when traffic reaches "eth0", it is already encapsulated with the VXLAN headers – it is no longer an ICMP packet!

How do we confirm this?

You can see traffic relevant to the tunnel, using a command as follows:

```
0:w1> tcpdump -i C0w1-eth0 port 8472
```

Now, if you run the ping, you will see some traffic here. But, how do we confirm that this is indeed the same ping packets being encapsulated. We can do that with the "tshark" command[6].

Aside: tshark is a command-line equivalent of the more famous Wireshark command. It is very useful for examining packet captures and flows with a lot of processing functionality on top.

Run the following command:

```
0:w1> tshark -V -d udp.port==8472,vxlan port 8472
```

In this, we:
1. "-V": run it in verbose mode
2. "-d udp.port==8472,vxlan": define that udp traffic on port 8462 be parsed as vxlan. (This is needed since the default port for vxlan is something else).
3. "port 8472": filter traffic only on this port. (We do this just to reduce the noise in the capture.)

The partial output of this command is:

```
Frame 1: 148 bytes on wire (1184 bits), 148 bytes captured (1184 bits)
on interface
  C0w1-eth0, id 0              [447/834]
    Interface id: 0 (C0w1-eth0)
      Interface name: C0w1-eth0
    Encapsulation type: Ethernet (1)
    Arrival Time: Mar  9, 2023 09:27:07.240587208 UTC
    [Time shift for this packet: 0.000000000 seconds]
    Epoch Time: 1678354027.240587208 seconds
    [Time delta from previous captured frame: 0.000000000 seconds]
    [Time delta from previous displayed frame: 0.000000000 seconds]
```

---

[6]https://tshark.dev/

```
   [Time since reference or first frame: 0.000000000 seconds]
   Frame Number: 1
   Frame Length: 148 bytes (1184 bits)
   Capture Length: 148 bytes (1184 bits)
   [Frame is marked: False]
   [Frame is ignored: False]                                    [433/834]
   [Protocols in frame: eth:ethertype:ip:udp:vxlan:eth:ethertype:
   ip:icmp:data]
Ethernet II, Src: 96:f2:c4:2d:e5:15 (96:f2:c4:2d:e5:15), Dst: 7e:f6:20:
08:f6:1f (7e:f6:20:08:f6:1f)
   Destination: 7e:f6:20:08:f6:1f (7e:f6:20:08:f6:1f)
      Address: 7e:f6:20:08:f6:1f (7e:f6:20:08:f6:1f)
      .... ..1. .... .... .... .... = LG bit: Locally administered
      address (this is NOT the factory default)
      .... ...0 .... .... .... .... = IG bit: Individual address (unicast)
   Source: 96:f2:c4:2d:e5:15 (96:f2:c4:2d:e5:15)
      Address: 96:f2:c4:2d:e5:15 (96:f2:c4:2d:e5:15)
      .... ..1. .... .... .... .... = LG bit: Locally administered
      address (this is NOT the factory default)
      .... ...0 .... .... .... .... = IG bit: Individual address (unicast)
   Type: IPv4 (0x0800)
Internet Protocol Version 4, Src: 10.0.0.3, Dst: 10.0.0.4       [421/834]
   0100 .... = Version: 4
   .... 0101 = Header Length: 20 bytes (5)
   Differentiated Services Field: 0x00 (DSCP: CS0, ECN: Not-ECT)
      0000 00.. = Differentiated Services Codepoint: Default (0)
      .... ..00 = Explicit Congestion Notification: Not ECN-Capable
      Transport (0)
   Total Length: 134
   Identification: 0xf1a5 (61861)
   Flags: 0x00
      0... .... = Reserved bit: Not set
      .0.. .... = Don't fragment: Not set
      ..0. .... = More fragments: Not set
      ...0 0000 0000 0000 = Fragment Offset: 0
   Time to Live: 64
   Protocol: UDP (17)                                           [407/834]
   Header Checksum: 0x74bb [validation disabled]
   [Header checksum status: Unverified]
   Source Address: 10.0.0.3
   Destination Address: 10.0.0.4
User Datagram Protocol, Src Port: 33642, Dst Port: 8472
```

```
        Source Port: 33642
        Destination Port: 8472
        Length: 114
        Checksum: 0x148a [unverified]
        [Checksum Status: Unverified]
        [Stream index: 0]
        [Timestamps]
            [Time since first frame: 0.000000000 seconds]
            [Time since previous frame: 0.000000000 seconds]        [393/834]
        UDP payload (106 bytes)
Virtual eXtensible Local Area Network
        Flags: 0x0800, VXLAN Network ID (VNI)
            0... .... .... .... = GBP Extension: Not defined
            .... 1... .... .... = VXLAN Network ID (VNI): True
            .... .... .0.. .... = Don't Learn: False
            .... .... .... 0... = Policy Applied: False
            .000 .000 0.00 .000 = Reserved(R): 0x0000
        Group Policy ID: 0
        VXLAN Network Identifier (VNI): 100
        Reserved: 0
Ethernet II, Src: e2:9d:37:d3:45:f3 (e2:9d:37:d3:45:f3), Dst: ea:4d:2d:
    69:23:e1 (ea:4d:2d:69:23:e1)                    [381/834]
        Destination: ea:4d:2d:69:23:e1 (ea:4d:2d:69:23:e1)
            Address: ea:4d:2d:69:23:e1 (ea:4d:2d:69:23:e1)
            .... ..1. .... .... .... .... = LG bit: Locally administered address
            (this is NOT the factory default)
            .... ...0 .... .... .... .... = IG bit: Individual address (unicast)
        Source: e2:9d:37:d3:45:f3 (e2:9d:37:d3:45:f3)
            Address: e2:9d:37:d3:45:f3 (e2:9d:37:d3:45:f3)
            .... ..1. .... .... .... .... = LG bit: Locally administered address
            (this is NOT the factory default)
            .... ...0 .... .... .... .... = IG bit: Individual address (unicast)
        Type: IPv4 (0x0800)
Internet Protocol Version 4, Src: 11.10.224.0, Dst: 11.11.176.2
        0100 .... = Version: 4
        .... 0101 = Header Length: 20 bytes (5)
        Differentiated Services Field: 0x00 (DSCP: CS0, ECN: Not-ECT)
            0000 00.. = Differentiated Services Codepoint: Default (0)
            .... ..00 = Explicit Congestion Notification: Not ECN-Capable
            Transport (0)
        Total Length: 84
        Identification: 0x3d10 (15632)
```

```
      Flags: 0x40, Don't fragment
          0... .... = Reserved bit: Not set
          .1.. .... = Don't fragment: Set
          ..0. .... = More fragments: Not set
      ...0 0000 0000 0000 = Fragment Offset: 0
      Time to Live: 63                                        [358/834]
      Protocol: ICMP (1)
      Header Checksum: 0x5881 [validation disabled]
      [Header checksum status: Unverified]
      Source Address: 11.10.224.0
      Destination Address: 11.11.176.2
Internet Control Message Protocol
      Type: 8 (Echo (ping) request)
      Code: 0
      Checksum: 0x8379 [correct]
      [Checksum Status: Good]
      Identifier (BE): 46077 (0xb3fd)
      Identifier (LE): 64947 (0xfdb3)
      Sequence Number (BE): 1 (0x0001)
      Sequence Number (LE): 256 (0x0100)
      Timestamp from icmp data: Mar  9, 2023 09:27:07.000000000 UTC
      [Timestamp from icmp data (relative): 0.240587208 seconds]
      Data (48 bytes)

0000   89 aa 03 00 00 00 00 00 10 11 12 13 14 15 16 17   ................
0010   18 19 1a 1b 1c 1d 1e 1f 20 21 22 23 24 25 26 27   ........ !"#$%&'
0020   28 29 2a 2b 2c 2d 2e 2f 30 31 32 33 34 35 36 37   ()*+,-./01234567
      Data: 89aa03000000000010111213141516171819191a1b1c1d1e1f202
            122232425262728292a2b?
      [Length: 48]
```

This shows one frame, which is a UDP packet on port 8472. Below this is the packet decoded, which is seen as a VXLAN packet. Note that the VNI is 100, which is what we setup in the Flannel config.

Inside the VXLAN packet is the actual payload, which contains an Ethernet frame with an IPv4 packet. This is how tunneling works – normal packets are encapsulated as payload into other packets on the underlay with the VXLAN header. Tshark has decoded this payload packet as well and shows that it is actually an ICMP packet!

See the source and destination IPs of the inner packet – these are the source and destination containers. Note the src and dest IPs of the outer packet – these are the worker IPs!

Exercise: Run this capture yourself and confirm that this is the same ICMP packet that you observe in the other higher level interfaces. Examine it at the source and destination IPs in the inner packet in the capture.

4.9 k8s-netsim: Exercises

Examine the Flannel logs in the "/tmp/knetsim" folder in the simulator environment.

Change the Flannel parameters, such as IP ranges, or VXLAN configuration such as VNI or port, and re-build and run the simulator. See that the changes are reflected in the simulator.

4.10 Summary

In this chapter, we looked at the CNI, the reason why it is needed, what the spec provides and how to use it. We then looked at one CNI plugin, Flannel, and saw how to run it in our simulator to achieve container–container networking.

5

Services

5.1 Introduction

In the last chapter we saw how individual containers can talk to each other. However, while it is needed, this is not enough to implement the service abstraction – to allow containers to talks to services.

It is important to outline what we will look at in this chapter. Here, we are only concerned with containers communicating with services within this cluster. Service–service communication is the backbone of all micro-service architecture solutions. In this chapter, we will not look at external communication with services in the cluster.

5.2 Technology: Kube-proxy and Kube-dns

Kubernetes depends on two key pieces of technologies to achieve this: "kube-proxy" and "kube-dns". *Kube-proxy*[1] is a network proxy that runs on each kubernetes node and manages the routing rules for the nodes. For example, kube-proxy rules are used to manage the load balancing of services hosted on those nodes. Kube-proxy works over iptables (which is the default mode) or ipvs (IP virtual server) which enables transport-layer load balancing capabilities.

---

[1]https://kubernetes.io/docs/concepts/overview/components/#kube-proxy

Figure 5.1: Typical architecture of kubeproxy in Kubernetes.

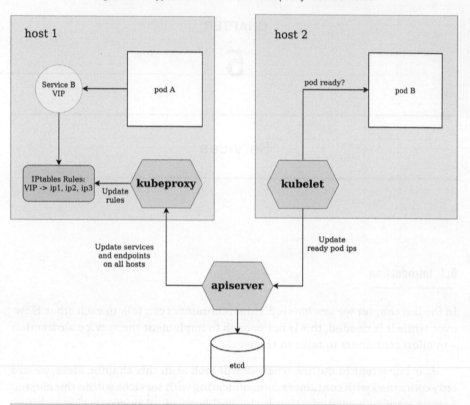

Kubernetes DNS[2] is used to identify services in the cluster by names instead of IP addresses. Kube-dns or CoreDNS as its known in recent Kubernetes versions listens for service related events and updates its record for the service end-point. It the updates the nameserver fields for all the new pods, which enables resolving the service request using the given name for the service.

Figure 5.1 shows a typical deployment of kube-proxy in Kubernetes. This component runs on each worker host and reprograms the local IPTables (or other such backends) to match the current reality of the pod deployment. As pods come up on other workers, individual kubelet services on those workers forward this information to the control plane which then messages kube-proxy running on all workers. Then, kube-proxy updates the local IPTables rules which are fired every time any local pod tries to address the service VIP. (Note that we have assumed ClusterIP model of deployment here, which is the default.

---

[2]https://kubernetes.io/docs/concepts/services-networking/dns-pod-service/

There are other models, such as NodePort which may involved no Virtual IP for services.)

5.3 k8s-netsim: Achieving Services

For the purpose of the simulator we shall only focus on the "kube-proxy" component and we shall not implement the "kube-dns" component. The chief reason for this is that DNS is a well known approach and the application of it in kubernetes is nothing out of the ordinary – unlike "kube-proxy" which is a more custom component.

While the real kube-proxy automatically manages service lifecycle dynamically (managing pod scale up/down and clean up of services when they are deleted), in the interest of simplicity, we shall only deal with static rules – and no automatic management of IPs or pod scale up.

In the simulator, we provide an interface to do this:

```
C0.kp_vip_add("100.64.10.1", ["c2", "c3"])
```

This interface does the following: declares containers c2 and c3 to form the backing pods of a service to be reachable at the virtual IP 100.64.10.1.

This is obviously different from the real model:

- In the real version, all pods in a deployment are automatically assumed to be endpoints for a service. Since, we don't model the "deployment" resource, we need to manually specify which pods are to be covered under a service. Note that the service creation shown above emulates the *Cluster IP* based service type.
- In the real version, services have names. This is especially needed since the DNS entries use this name to allow other pods to access this service. Since, we don't implement DNS in our simulator, we skip naming services.
- In the real version, "kube-proxy" automatically assigns VIPs and manages the IP space. Here, for simplicity, we manually select the VIP to be used.

How does the simulator implement this interface? While kube-proxy uses IPTables, we internally use "nftables" to achieve the same. In the next dew sections we shall go into details of nftables.

5.4 Introduction to Nftables

Nftables[3] is the next generation replacement for iptables. It is an in-kernel network packet classification virtual machine which handles operations like connection tracking, NAT, and socket queuing. For configuration, a userspace command line tool *nft* is provided with it. A high-level user library *libnftables* is also available that has support for json based input configuration. Nftables has been around from 2014 but has only recently been adopted widely and also is a go-to solution for firewall rules.

Even though it has features that look similar to iptables in terms of rules, there are benefits of nftables over iptables:

- Unification: With iptables you had different tables to add rules for ipv4 and ipv6. With nftables you can have one solution managing ipv4, ipv6, arptables, etc.
- Flexibility: Similar to iptables, nftables supports chaining of rules. However, it does not start with a base chain and hence provides flexibility.
- Performance: With iptables, even if the rules do not match a flow, it needs to be verified for each rule which adds unnecessary overhead. Nftables uses maps and concatenation to structure the ruleset.

Figure 5.2 shows a high level view of how nftables compares to IPTables if you are familiar with the older tool. The kernel modules implementing the

Figure 5.2: NFT modules in user and kernel space.

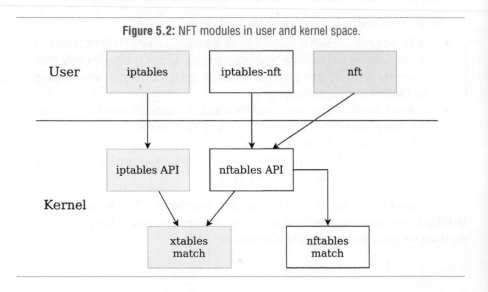

---

[3]https://www.nftables.org

actual processing of packets are completely different, as is the API layer. However, to help users move their older scripts, a compatibility tool iptables-nft has been provided which can run older IPTable format rules with the newer nftables plumbing.

5.5 Hands-on: Nftables

In this section, we shall play with "nftables" to demonstrate its use. As before, start up a fresh instance of the simulator container:

```
$ docker run -it --privileged --rm --entrypoint bash knetsim
```

The environment already comes with the "nftables" installed for use.

First, let us check the existing rules:

```
$ nft list ruleset
```

As expected, it will be empty. (Note that the simulator is not running in this setup.)

For a full list of nft commands, refer to the official reference page[4].

Rules in "nft" are organized in chains which are placed inside tables. So, we start with creating tables first.

```
$ nft add table ip table1
```

This creates a new table "table1" meant to handle ip family type. The allowed family types are: "arp", "bridge", "ip", "ip6", "inet", "netdev".

You can check the new (empty) table exists using the command as before:

```
$ nft list ruleset
table ip table1 {
}
```

---

[4]https://wiki.nftables.org/wiki-nftables/index.php/Main_Page

Now, let us create a chain:

```
nft add chain ip table1 chain1 { type filter hook output priority
0 \; policy accept \; }
```

This command does a number of things:

- We refer to the existing table1 of the ip family.
- We create a new chain with the name "chain1".
- This new chain is declared to be of type "filter". The allowed options here are: "filter" to conditionally drop packets, "nat" to perform address translations and "route" to modify route lookups. In this example, we will use the "filter" type.
- Hook specifies which hook point we will attach this chain to. Refer to Figure 5.3 later in this chapter to see all available hook points. Hook points are very important to select – using the wrong hook point, you may miss processing the packets you want to process. In this example, we will use the "output" hook point. Not all hook points make sense for all types.
- We add a priority for this chain (in comparison to other chains attached to the same hook point). All chains are processed, but in order of priority. We use a priority 0 in this example, although anything would have worked since we don't have any other chains. Priorities can be specified as numbers (which can be negative also) or predefined names associated with specific priorities. All this information can be found in the main pages.
- We attach a default policy to accept (can be dropped otherwise). This is what will be done if no rule in this chain matches the incoming packet.

Now "list ruleset" as before and check that the newly created chain has been loaded into the table.

Now, we have a table and a chain, but nothing useful can happen without a rule. So, let us create a new rule:

```
nft add rule ip table1 chain1 ip daddr 9.9.9.9 counter
```

As may be obvious, the command has the following parts to it:

- We add a new rule to our existing chain1 in table1 of the family ip.
- We have a match condition, "ip daddr 9.9.9.9", which basically checks the destination IP of a packet and compares it to "9.9.9.9" which is an open DNS service offered by IBM[5]. (This is comparable to Google DNS 8.8.8.8 or Cloudflare's DNS 1.1.1.1.)
- Finally, we have the statement, in this case "counter". Counter maintains a simple counter that is incremented for every packet that matches the condition.

You have seen the main components of a rule: a match condition and the statement.

---

[5]https://www.quad9.net/

Match conditions can reference anything in the packet: header fields at different layers, lengths of fields, checksums, etc. For a full listing see the reference[6].

Statements are usually one of the following:

- Verdict statements: accept, drop, continue, return, jump, goto, queue (to a userspace function). These are meant to be control flow like statements to decide how to manage a packet.
- Counter: to simply count passing packets.
- Limit: rate limiting packets.
- Nat: to dnat or snat packets.

Now, let us check our rule. Counters should be empty:

```
$ nft list ruleset
table ip table1 {
    chain chain1 {
        type filter hook output priority filter; policy accept;
        ip daddr 9.9.9.9 counter packets 0 bytes 0
    }
}
```

Send a single ping packet:

```
$ ping -c 1 9.9.9.9
```

Check the counters again. It should look like the following:

```
$ nft list ruleset
table ip table1 {
    chain chain1 {
        type filter hook output priority filter; policy accept;
        ip daddr 9.9.9.9 counter packets 1 bytes 84
    }
}
```

The single packet has been matched and acted upon.

To delete rules, we need to use handles. First, list rules with handles:

---

[6]https://wiki.nftables.org/wiki-nftables/index.php/Quick_reference-nftables_in_10_minutes#Matches

```
$ nft -a list ruleset
table ip table1 { # handle 306
    chain chain1 { # handle 1
        type filter hook output priority filter; policy accept;
        ip daddr 9.9.9.9 counter packets 2 bytes 168 # handle 2
    }
}
```

Delete the rule using the handle:

```
nft delete rule ip table1 chain1 handle 2
```

List the ruleset and confirm that this rule has been dropped.

Deleting chains and tables is a lot easier:

```
nft delete chain ip table1 chain1
nft delete table ip table1
```

Now that you know how to create and delete nft elements, play around with the nft command.

As an exercise, add a rule to "drop" packets to this IP and then try pinging. It should no longer work.

Nftables has a lot of other features that we do not cover here, features that make it much more powerful than IPTables. These include:

- Intervals to support ranges of IPs like "192.168.0.1–192.168.0.250" or ports "1–1024".
- Concatenation syntax to work on pairs of structures like (IP . port).
- Math operations like hashing, number series.
- Sets and maps: data structures to help decouple rules from the data it operates on.
- Quotas: rules that match only until a number of bytes have passed.
- Flowtables: network stack bypass, to move packets to userspace programs for out-of-kernel custom processing.

Earlier in this section, we talked about hook points. Now is a good time to revist these. Figure 5.3 shows the Netfilter hook points in the Linux kernel with a focus only on the IP layer. One way to understand hook points is that they are places in the kernel's networking stack where you can stop, inspect and act on packets, such as modify packets or control their flow. We have seen use of nft in this chapter to manipulate packets using these hook points, but there are other mechanism which rely on these hook points, for e.g., eBPF programs can be run at these hook points.

44

Figure 5.3: Netfilter hook points in the kernel – focus only on the IP layer.

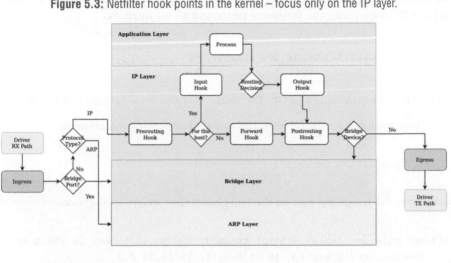

There are mainly five hook points:

- Prerouting: For all packets coming into the system, even before routing decisions are taken. Useful for early filtering or making changes that would impact routing.
- Input: For packets headed to the local machined, that is, where the destination is an application running on this machine.
- Forward: Packets going to be forwarded to some other machine.
- Output: Packets generated by local apps.
- Postrouting: All packets leaving the local machine.

There are similar hook points in the ARP layer, not shown. As we mentioned earlier, not all operation types make sense for all hook points. For a full version of this diagram, refer to the official documentation on hook points[7].

5.6 k8s-netsim: Implementing Kube-proxy

Internally, the simulator implements the kube-proxy feature using a simple approach, as detailed below.

On startup, we create a table and chain set to the hook point prerouting – for packets originating from within pods. Similarly, we create a table and chain

---

[7]https://wiki.nftables.org/wiki-nftables/index.php/Netfilter_hooks

attached to the hook point output – for packets originating on the hosts. We also add an IP route using the following command on all workers:

```
ip route add 100.64.0.0/16 dev flannel.100
```

to route packets destined to our VIP range into the local flannel interface.

Then, for each new service added to our cluster with the command:

```
C0.kp_vip_add("100.64.10.1", ["c2", "c3"])
```

we create the following rule in the two chains that we created above:

```
nft add rule ip <table> <chain> ip daddr 100.64.10.1 dnat to jhash ip
    checksum mod 2 map {0: 11.11.0.2, 1: 11.15.48.2 }
```

This rule does a number of things:
- First we lookup the pod ips of the two containers we want to target as backend – "c2" and "c3". In this example, we have the ips – "11.11.0.2" and "11.15.48.2".
- We construct a map out of these values, inline in the rule, with keys being 0, 1 and so on.
- The rule match condition is "ip daddr 100.64.10.1" which matches packets with this destination IP. This is what we want since this VIP doesn't actually exist anywhere else.
- The statement we apply to this is "dnat" – destination NAT to something. But what IP should we use?
- The part of the rule: "jhash ip checksum mod 2" takes the checksum field of the packet and hashes it and finally applies mod 2 to the result – with the output being 0 or 1 randomly.
- We then lookup the map to convert this number to an IP. This IP is used to forward the packet.

So, all in all, we construct a new rule for every service that randomly chooses one of the specified backends to send packets to.

You may notice that multiple packets of the same flow should be sent to the same destination, otherwise the basic structure of the connection does not hold. This is already happening – the nat hook point only applies to the first packet of a new flow – subsequent packets automatically follow the processing of the first one. So, we do not have to do anything further to ensure correct working.

Now that we have the service specifies, as an exercise:
- Ping the service IP from container c1 and check that it works.
- Delete one of the two containers c2/c3 and see what happens when you ping the VIP. (Hint: try to run the ping command a few times in succession.)

As further exercise, you can try out the following:

- Create a few more containers and expose them using a new VIP.
- Examine the nft rules that are added to the workers.
- Go through the code and understand how the nft rules are being generated. Specifically see which hook points are being used.

6

Exposing Services

6.1 Introduction

In the last chapter, we got the service abstraction up and running for pods in the cluster. Although a lot of inter-service communication happens, the micro-service graph is first activiated, or the whole process really starts, from an external request.

In this chapter, we will see how services can be exposed out of the cluster.

6.2 Ingress

The concept in Kubernetes that allows exposing services is called Ingress. Ingress[1] allows you to expose HTTP or HTTPS services under a single url on different paths.

For example, consider a simple social network like an application developed and deployed using the micro-service pattern. It could have several micro-services such as:

- users: to manage registration and login of users
- posts: to manage creation, updation and deletion of posts
- db: data base to store all information
- frontend: actual web ui servicing end users.

---

[1]https://kubernetes.io/docs/concepts/services-networking/ingress/

Even in this very simple example (real micro-service deployments can go to hundreds of micro-services), you can observe some things about service communication:

- You want all services to be able to talk to each other. (This is what we achieved in the last chapter.)
- You want the frontend service to be the default exposed service that users access when they go to the website url.
- The users and posts services should be exposed as APIs that can be called from the frontend Web ui.
- You don't want to expose your db service under any circumstances.

This is where Ingress comes in. You may need to specify your Ingress resource something like in Listing 7.1.

```
apiVersion: networking.k8s.io/v1
kind: Ingress
metadata:
  name: minimal—ingress
  annotations:
    nginx.ingress.kubernetes.io/rewrite—target: /
spec:
  ingressClassName: nginx—example
  rules:
  - http:
      paths:
      - path: /
        pathType: Exact
        backend:
          service:
            name: frontend
            port:
              number: 80
      - path: /users
        pathType: Prefix
        backend:
          service:
            name: users
            port:
              number: 80
      - path: /posts
        pathType: Prefix
        backend:
          service:
            name: posts
```

```
port:
  number: 8000
```
Listing 6.1: Example Ingress YAML

This Ingress specifies a number of things:

- The frontend service is exposed onto the external path "/" as an exact match. This is the only path that will get access to the frontend service. Also, port 80 of the service is used.
- The users services is exposed on the external path "/users" as a Prefix. So, urls like "<websiteurl>/users/create" and "<websiteurl>/users/login" will all automatically map to the underlying service at port 80.
- Similarly with the post service, except we route traffic to port 8000 of the underlying service.

Hopefully, this gives you an example of how Ingress is useful. However, just specifying an Ingress resource is not enough, it has to be implemented by an IngressController setup in the cluster. Though Kubernetes does not come out of the box with an Ingress Controller, there exists a number of controller providers[2].

How do these Ingress controllers work? They typically wrap an existing third party technology like HAProxy, Nginx, Traefik, etc and program the underlying tool using the given configuration. Typically, they translate the provided Ingress YAML into a format suitable for the underlying tool.

This is because these tools – many predating Kubernetes – are all well established projects that focus on the key use case of acting as a service frontend, doing things like TLS termination, load balancing, ingress security controls, authentication, etc. Thus, they are well suited to play the role of the Ingress implementor.

6.3 k8s-simulator: Exposing Services

As you may have guessed by now, we statically configure one of these tools to implement Ingress like functionality in our simulator. The tool we have chosen is nginx[3].

Nginx calls itself a HTTP and reverse proxy server with a number of features needed for HTTP serving and tools to programmatically process requests. It is a very well established tool and serves a large part of the internet.

---

[2]https://kubernetes.io/docs/concepts/services-networking/ingress-controllers/
[3]https://nginx.org/en/

Figure 6.1: Exposing two services under a single endpoint using Ingress.

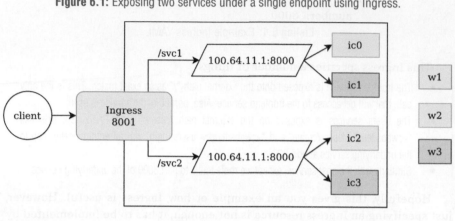

As before, we have a programmatic API:

```
CO.get("w1").run_ingress("grp1", 8001,
  [{"path": "/svc1", "endpoint": "100.64.11.1:8000"},
   {"path": "/svc2", "endpoint": "100.64.11.2:8000"}])
```

where we:

- Run an ingress on worker w1 of C0 at port 8001.
- Exposes two services under the two paths.
- The underlying service is referred to using the service VIPs we used in the last chapter. Note that if we had a DNS set up, we could use simple names and ports.

Figure 6.1 shows the Ingress setup we will achieve with the code above.

Assuming this works for the moment, you may have a question of how do we test this? So far, our services have been simple empty containers and we only ever pinged them. But, now we need to setup some sort of HTTP service to verify that expose works.

To this end, we have included a simple HTTP server that serves a hardcoded string in the simulator (in the path "utils/ss.py". So, to enable the two service above, we use code like the following:

```
# Setup containers for ingress
CO.get("w2").create_container("ic0")
CO.get("w2").exec_container_async("ic0", "./utils/ss.py S1-W2")
CO.get("w3").create_container("ic1")
```

```
CO.get("w3").exec_container_async("ic1", "./utils/ss.py S1-W3")
CO.kp_vip_add("100.64.11.1", ["ic0", "ic1"])
CO.get("w2").create_container("ic2")
CO.get("w2").exec_container_async("ic2", "./utils/ss.py S2-W2")
CO.get("w3").create_container("ic3")
CO.get("w3").exec_container_async("ic3", "./utils/ss.py S2-W3")
CO.kp_vip_add("100.64.11.2", ["ic2", "ic3"])
```

What are we doing here?

- Create container ic0 on worker 2 which returns the string "S1-W2".
- Create container ic1 on worker 3 which returns the string "S1-W3".
- Create a service that encapsulates containers ic0 and ic1.

Then we do the same thing with another service.

There is a caveat here: normally replicas of a service are identical in all aspects. Here we return two different strings from the two replicas – is this really a service? We do this just for demonstration purposes so that it is easy to show the requests going to two different replicas.

Internally, our simulator runs nginx with a generated config that looks like the following:

```
events{}
http {
  server {
    listen 8001;
    location /svc1 { proxy_pass http://100.64.11.1:8000; }
    location /svc2 { proxy_pass http://100.64.11.2:8000; }
  }
}
```

This is an "nginx.conf" file conforming to the standard format expected by nginx. For more details, you can refer to the official nginx configuration.

6.4 k8s-simulator: Hands-on

First access the service using its VIP from worker 1.

```
mininet> C0w1 curl 100.64.11.1:8000
S1-W2
```

If you run this a few times, you should see one of the two responses "S1-W2" and "S1-W3". This is exactly as we saw in the last chapter – basic service implementation.

Now, let us access the same service via the Ingress, from the same worker node:

```
mininet> C0w1 curl localhost:8001/svc1
S1-W2
```

Run it a few times and verify that the behavior is ok. Now, also try reaching the "/svc2" path and check if it works as expected.

So, this is Ingress working. However, we haven't proven that it is accessible from outside. Let us do that now.

First check the IP of the worker 1 host:

```
mininet> C0w1 hostname -I
10.0.0.3 ...
```

You can try now reaching this IP from outside, say the e1 node (which is not a Kubernetes worker at all):

```
mininet> C0e1 curl 10.0.0.3:8001/svc1
S1-W2
```

This is the Ingress working correctly as expected. Just to summarize the flow, now:

- Client on e1 connects to the nginx ingress exposed at 8001.
- Nginx on worker 1 rerouted the request to the Service VIP 100.64.11.1 port 8000.
- Our kube-proxy equivalent (based on nftables) translates the VIP to one of the real backing pod IPs.
- Flannel routes the request to the correct location based on the pod ip.

You can see how the concepts we have introduced in each chapter have built on top of the previous one.

CHAPTER

7

Mutli-cluster Networking

7.1 Introduction

In the previous section we saw how services can be exposed outside of a cluster. While that is useful for interactions between end users and services running on a cluster, it does not scale to the most generic use cases of multi-cluster applications.

What are these multi-cluster or multi-cloud applications? Why are they the future?

While a single cluster of machines scales and scales well – it has certain limitations. All worker nodes are within a single zone in a datacenter.

Having multiple clusters is going to be the norm rather than the exception in the coming future.

- An application will run across multiple clouds (from the same or different providers) for the purpose of geo-distribution. Note that this is different from simple sharding, where each data center caters to one section of users. This involves app micro services in multiple clouds talking to each other to synchronize state etc.
- A lot of deployments are hybrid-cloud: some portion of the app runs on public cloud providers and some on internal enterprise data centers. These portions run on the internal sites are typically the crown jewels – due to security, proprietery hardware or other requirements. In these cases, there would be a certain amount of communication between these two clouds in the normal workflows.

Figure 7.1: Example of a multi-cloud scenario spanning multiple public clouds, private clouds and edge clouds.

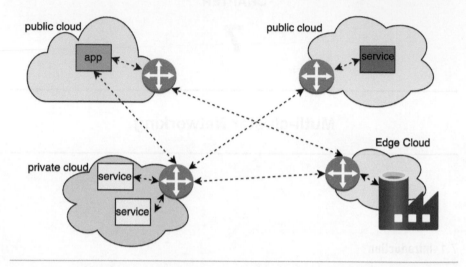

- Edge/Telco clouds are an emerging field – where Kubernetes clusters are run close to the end user. Some amount of latency sensitive processing is best offloaded to such clouds; however these clouds will have limited resources, such as computing and storage, and thus cannot run entire cloud apps. This is yet another scenario where enabling cross-cloud networking is a must.

Given this new world and applications spanning multiple clusters, we need solutions that manage networking between pods and services running on multiple clusters.

- Routing: how to find a pathway between a container on one cluster and another.
- Management: how to manage networking as pods/services come up and go on different clusters.
- Security: securing cross-cluster traffic that may flow over the internet.
- Policies: which pods/services can talk to which other pods/services.

Clearly, all of these are problems faced within a single cluster too, but, as we saw, there are several layers for in-cluster networking and several tools for each layer that solve these problems.

7.2 Multi-cluster Networking

In this chapter, we want to achieve the blue line shown in Figure 7.2. That is, we have multiple clusters connected with some sort of underlay that connects them;

Figure 7.2: Extending our simulator to allow pods to talk between clusters. We want to achieve the blue line in this chapter.

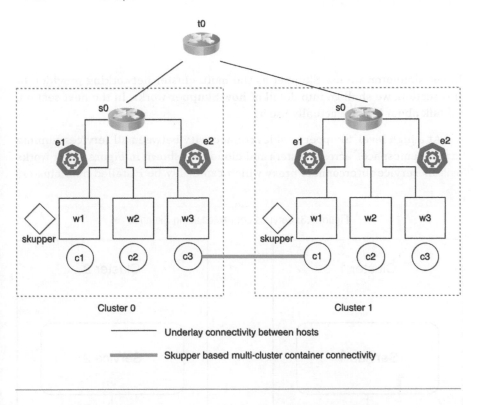

thus workers can talk between clusters if needed, although they will typically be behind a firewall and not allowed to freely communicate. Each cluster is an independent solution – none of the lower layers that we have discussed up until now should be changed.

As we saw in the previous chapters, we rely on some existing solution and adapt it for our simulation. So, what do we do now?

As of the time of the writing of this book, multi-cluster networking is still an open problem. There are a number of different solutions, all focused on different trade-offs, and none of them have satisfactory solved all dimensions of the problem.

Some example solutions include: Cilium Multi-cluster[1], Istio[2], Consul Multi-cluster[3], Submariner[4], Skupper[5], etc.

7.3 Skupper

In our simulator, we use Skupper as the multi-cluster networking provider. In this section, we shall go into detail of how Skupper works. In the next section, we talk about how we actually use it.

At a high level, Skupper enables connectivity between all services running in two namespaces across clusters and clouds. As shown in Figure 7.3, it works as a L7 service interconnect proxy which can easily be installed onto clusters

Figure 7.3: Services connected using Skupper.

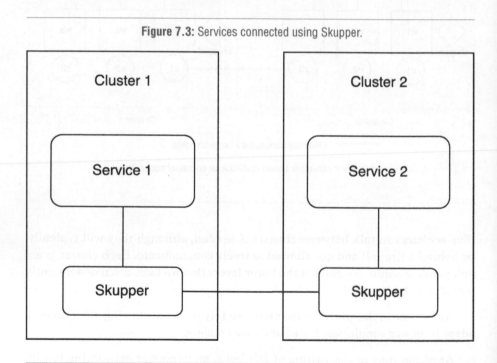

[1]https://docs.cilium.io/en/stable/network/clustermesh/
[2]https://istio.io/latest/docs/ops/configuration/traffic-management/multicluster/
[3]https://www.consul.io/docs/k8s/installation/multi-cluster
[4]https://github.com/submariner-io/submariner
[5]https://skupper.io/index.html

without any low-level changes to the networking setup. All inter cluster communication is secured using mutual TLS and Skupper does not need any admin privileges on the clusters it works on.

7.4 k8s-netsim: Multi-cluster Networking

How do we simulate multi-cluster networking?

First, we simulate multiple clusters by instantiating multiple copies of the cluster object we have been using so far. Each cluster has all the pieces we have talked about in this book. Finally, to establish the underlay, we connect each cluster's top level switches into a single higher level switch. Thus, workers from all cluster can reach workers from other clusters via this switch.

Now, we run Skupper to achieve multi-cluster connectivity. As before, we build a static configuration for Skupper instead of running the full dynamic version. Specifically, the Skupper project consists of the following components:

- Skupper router: to do the actual routing
- Site controller: to manage links between various clusters
- Service controller: to manage exposure of services as they come up/go down.

In our simulator, we only run a Skupper-router setup with generated config files. We don't use the other components at all.

What does this configuration file look like?

Each file starts out with a section as follows:

```
"router", {
  "id": "c0",
  "mode": "interior",
  "helloMaxAgeSeconds": "3",
  "metadata": "{\"id\":\"c0\",\"version\":\"1.0.2\"}"
}
```

where we identify the name of the Skupper router. We have one router per cluster (which we run on workern1). The mode is identified to be "interior" or "edge" – the only difference being that edge routers terminate the routing graph don't connect outward to any other routers. In our usecase, we mark every cluster as an "interior" router.

Every router has a listener:

```
"listener",
{
    "name": "interior-listener",
    "role": "inter-router",
    "port": 55671,
    "maxFrameSize": 16384,
    "maxSessionFrames": 640
}
```

to be able to connect to other routers.

We also have, on some routers, connectors configured:

```
"connector",
{
    "name": "link1",
    "role": "inter-router",
    "host": "<ip of remote>",
    "port": "55671",
    "cost": 1,
    "maxFrameSize": 16384,
    "maxSessionFrames": 640
}
```

Note how the port set in the connector is the port used as the listener in the remote. This section in the config tell the Skupper router to form a link with a remote Skupper router with some config parameters. The "cost" parameter can be used to setup weights for the links, for example.

Now that we have seen the config elements relevant to connecting clusters, how are services exposed and consumed? Much like the "listener" and "connector" sections we saw just now, Skupper also has "tcpConnector" and "tcpListener" which look like the following.

On a cluster, where we have a service that needs to be exposed, on that router we add a config as follows:

```
"tcpConnector",
{
    "name": "backend",
```

```
    "host": "localhost",
    "port": "8090",
    "address": "backend:8080",
    "siteId": "c1"
}
```

Where we indicate to the Skupper (on site c1) that it should create a new service with the address of "backend:8080" (a string identifier) and connect to "host" and "port" for the actual service. The "name" is only used to differentiate between tcpConnectors on the router. Note how, we have set the address to refer to a different port (purely for illustration purpose. Instead of this, we can use normal strings as well).

Then, on other remote locations, we have the following configuration:

```
"tcpListener",
{
    "name": "backend:8080",
    "port": "1028",
    "address": "backend:8080",
    "siteId": "c0"
}
```

which on the Skupper router for cluster c0 creates a new local port 1028 to reach the service tagged with the address "backend:8080". What this does, is setup the underlying Skupper network to enable local services to reach the <local skupper ip>:1028 and get routed to the remote service on cluster c1.

We use the same principles shown above to generate configuration files.

Now, in our setup:

- The "host" in the "tcpConnector" would be service VIP. The "port" would be the port exposed by the service.
- The Skupper routers are running on worker 1 of each cluster. So, any service exposed on Skupper (using the "port" in the "tcpListener"), would simply be reachable from any pod in the cluster by using the worker IP.

We set up the Skupper portions in our simulator using code that looks like the following:

```
# start a service in a container
C0.get("w3").exec_container_async("c4", "python3 -m http.server 80")
ip = C0.got("w3").exec_container("c4", "hostname -I").split()[0]
```

```
svcs = [{"name": "svc1", "cluster": "0", "host": ip, "port": "80",
"lport": 1028}]

create_conf(C0, remotes=[], svcs=svcs)
create_conf(C1, [C0], svcs=svcs)
C0.start_skupper()
C1.start_skupper()

# allow time for skupper to stabilize
time.sleep(5)

print("Run multi-cluster connectivity test...")
ip = C1.get("w1").IP()
print(C1.get("w2").exec_container("c2", "wget http://{0}:{1}".
format(ip, 1028)))
```

In this code snippet, we do the following:

- Run a server in a container on worker 3 of cluster 0.
- Obtain the pod ip of this container.
- Build a conf entry for a service using this information. You can see all relevant information present to build a Skupper conf file later on.
- We create the conf files for two skupper routers, one for each cluster. We specify what remotes we need to connect (C1 connects to C0 in this example) and what services we need to support. Based on the given information, different entries ("tcpConnectors" and "tcpListeners") are created in the different config files.
- We finally start up the Skupper routers using the given conf files. We wait for a while for the daemons to come up, the links to form, etc.
- Finally, on cluster 1, from worker 2, we "wget" to the worker1 ip, at 1028 port, which is where our service is exposed. When this works, the connection is made through the two Skupper routers to the actual container on cluster 0. So, the connection sequence is: C1-w2 -> C1-skupper (on w1) -> C0-skupper (on w1) -> C0-w3 (where the actual container is run).

Understand the steps above and run your own wget checks to verify that the connectivity is working. Now, there are a number of exercises you can do here:

- Look at the generated Skupper conf files in the "/tmp/knetsim/skupper" directory in the simulator environment.
- We exposed a pod IP instead of a service VIP for simplicity, but, based on your understanding of the previous chapters, it should be easy to see how multi-cluster connectivity would work with either service VIPs or Ingress. Check your understanding by modifying the code above to work in one of those two modes.

- Follow the flow of the packets, using tcpdump and tshark as shown above. Note: this can be challenging with the way Skupper works in encapsulating packets. Look into the AMQP network protocol for documentation on how the links between clusters are managed.
- Extend the setup to have more clusters. Try out different topologies, or update the code to change link weights and follow the packet flow.

7.5 Summary

In this section, we got a taste, a sample, of how multi-cluster networking is implemented.

8

Retrospective

> The more I learn, the more I realize
> how much I don't know.
>
> Albert Einstein

We are at the end of the deep-dive. Hopefully you learnt a thing or two!

Let us recap what we have learnt in this book.

- We simulated a simplified version of Kubernetes networking on the Mininet platform, using real tools wherever possible.
- We started out by running workers as Mininet hosts and simulating containers using network namespaces. To do this effectively, we explored network namespaces which underpins all of containet technology using the "ip netsns" tool.
- We then enabled pod-to-pod connectivity using the Flannel CNI plugin. We understood the way Flannel is configured and followed the lifecycle of the packets through the cross host VXLAN tunnel.
- We then looked at the Service abstraction and simulated a simplified kube-proxy that allows us to access replicas pods of a service behind a single virtual IP. To do this, we explored the "nftables" tool which is a powerhouse of its own and useful in a wide range of scenarios.
- We then followed up services with exposing them outside the cluster. We simulated Ingress in typical Kubernetes clusters using nginx, yet another standard solution.
- Finally, we took a first step into the emerging world of multi-cluster networking using Skupper. We setup cross cluster connectivity by manually configuring "Skupper-router" to proxy connections between two of our simulated clusters.

Hopefully, this hands-on approach has given you a peek under the hood of the complex machine that is Kubernetes. Where to from here?

- Alhough we have nudged the reader to look into the full code of the simulator, this may be a point to reinforce the suggestion. You understand most of it already.
- For simplicity, we omitted several variants of the technologies shown. For example, we did not explore how a DNS is used in Kubernetes. Similarly, we only looked at the IPTables variant of kube-proxy (which is the most common) and not at the others such as IPVS based services. We only explored the VXLAN tunneling approach to cross worker connectivity, though a lot of other options are available. We hope that this introduction will allow you to confidently approach these variants.
- We didn't go into the more advanced functionalities possible in each layer. Now may be a time to explore features such as connection security (using encryption), policies, observability, etc.
- In this book, we didn't explore the space of service meshes — mainly in the interests of simplicity. We invite the reader to explore the space and understand how it fits with the layers shown. The enterprising reader is invited to think about how we can extend the simulator we have built to demonstrate service meshes in a simple manner, and contribute back to our open-source simulator.
- Now that you have a solid grasp of the fundamentals that underpin them, take a second look at the Kubernetes and CNCF ecosystem. We suggest you approach the projects layer by layer as we have shown here: starting from container engines to CNI plugins to Ingress Controllers and finally to multi-cluster solutions. There are many alternatives that work at each layer offering various features, though the basics remain the same.

Happy journey!

Index

C

cloud native networking, 6
containers, 6, 7, 15, 21, 22, 24, 37, 52, 65

K

kubernetes, 6, 9, 37, 49, 50

M

multi cloud networking, ix
mininet 12, 13, 14, 54

C

cloud native ontwikkeling 6

containers 6, 7, 15, 21, 22, 24, 37, 52, 65

K

Kubernetes 6, 9, 37, 49, 50

M

multi cloud verwerken IV

minutes 1, 13, 14, 54